The Wisdom of Fishing

*The Truth, Passion, and
Philosophy of Man's
Favorite Sport*

CHRISTOPHER
ARMOUR

FOXGLOVE PRESS

The Wisdom of Fishing by Christopher Armour

 Published by Foxglove Press
1-877-205-1932
© 2004 Foxglove Press

ISBN 1-882959-53-1

Design by Armour&Armour, Nashville, Tennessee

First Edition 2004
1 2 3 4 5 6 7 8 9 10

To Daddy Pete,
who taught me
to fish

Contents

Introduction

Nearly fifty years later, I remember every detail about the day I learned to fish.

"Son, let's go fishing," said my grandfather, Daddy Pete. "We're gonna need some bait."

He led me out behind the barn under the big oak tree. I remember the moist smell of the leaves slowly composting, the sound the shovel made as it slid into the dark soil, the sight of the big fat worms we unearthed.

We pulled out a handful and headed for the garage to get our poles. The old canes seemed enormous, towering over my head. We set off down the hill.

Daddy Pete taught me about the hook, the line, the bobber. He showed me how to slide the worm over the hook, how to cast my line, how to watch for a bite.

"Now what?" I asked.

He smiled. "We wait."

The Wisdom of Fishing

Grasshoppers buzzed in the summer heat. Somewhere a bobwhite sang. Every now and then a big truck blew past on the highway.

Suddenly the bobber dunked, I yanked, and soon I had my first catch, a fat catfish. He wasn't the only one who was hooked.

Years later, my thoughts still go back to that hot drowsy day, the grassy bank beside a quiet pond, the young boy and an old man. And it strikes me that this is the essence of fishing. This is why it doesn't matter what you catch, or if you catch anything at all. This is why we keep going back to that green bank.

Maybe it's the solitude, maybe it's the purity of nature, maybe it's the waiting and thinking . . . but anglers have developed a distinct philosophy of fishing.

Introduction

In these pages you'll find a compendium of fishing wisdom, frequently funny and always insightful observations about the sport and its followers.

This book explores the fisherman's loose relationship with the truth. It takes a look at the strange habits and behaviors of anglers (particularly fly-fishers), their fetish for gear, their long-suffering wives. You'll find that fishermen have opinions about everything: who they are, when they should go fishing, why they go in the first place. And they know it's not the catching that's important—it's the time to worship in the church of fishing, the way the sport makes them whole that keeps them coming back.

I hope you find a few laughs, some food for thought, a satisfaction in being part of the family of anglers. And keep on fishing!

The Truth About Fishing

No other sport
has a looser
relationship
with the truth—
or with rulers

The Wisdom of Fishing

FISH IS supposed to be good for the brain, but fishing is even better for the imagination.

IF ALL the big fish that got away were in the sea, there wouldn't be any room for the water.

A FISHERMAN first lies in wait for a fish, and then lies in weight after landing it.

The ability to lie differs among people. For instance, a short-armed fisherman isn't as big a liar as a long-armed one.

THE BIGGEST fish he ever caught were those that got away.

EUGENE FIELD

NOTHING grows faster than a fish from the time it bites to the time it gets away.

NOTHING makes a fish bigger than almost being caught.

Do not tell fish
stories where the people
know you; but particularly,
don't tell them where
they know the fish.

MARK TWAIN

FLY FISHERMEN are born honest, but they get over it.

ED ZERN

FISHING is a delusion entirely surrounded by liars in old clothes.

DON MARQUIS

I GET ALL the truth I need in the newspaper every morning, and every chance I get I go fishing, or swap stories with fishermen, to get the taste of it out of my mouth.

ED ZERN

The Truth About Fishing

I fish, therefore I lie.

TOM CLARK

The Wisdom of Fishing

OF ALL THE liars among mankind,
the fisherman is the most trustworthy.

WILLIAM SHERWOOD FOX

ANGLERS . . . exaggerate grossly and
make gentle and inoffensive crea-
tures sound like wounded
buffalo and man-eating tigers.

RODERICK HAIG-BROWN

BRAGGING MAY not bring happiness,
but no man having caught a large fish
goes home through an alley.

Truth is stranger
than fishin'.

JIMMY BUFFETT

PEOPLE are under the impression that all that is required to make a good fisherman is the ability to tell lies easily and without blushing; but this is a mistake. Mere bald fabrication is useless; the veriest tyro can manage that. It is in the circumstantial detail, the embellishing touches of probability, the general air of scrupulous—almost of pedantic—veracity, that the experienced angler is seen.

JEROME K. JEROME

Fishing is like sex:
The less you get
the more you lie.

Record Catches

Species	Average Weight	Record Weight
Bass, Largemouth	2-3 lb.	22 lb., 4 oz.
Bass, Smallmouth	1-1½ lb.	11 lb., 15 oz.
Bass, White	1-2 lb.	5 lb., 14 oz.
Bluegill	½ lb.	4 lb., 12 oz.
Carp	1-6 lb.	57 lb., 13 oz.
Catfish, Blue	2-5 lb.	97 lb.
Catfish, Channel	1-2 lb.	58 lb.
Catfish, White	1-2 lb.	22 lb.
Crappie, Black	½ - 1 lb.	5 lb., 1 oz.
Crappie, White	½ - 1 lb.	5 lb., 3 oz.
Dolly Varden	½ - 2 lb.	8 lb., 1 oz.
Gar, Alligator	50-100 lb.	279 lb.
Gar, Longnose	10-25 lb.	50 lb, 5oz.
Muskellunge	15-25 lb.	69 lb., 15 oz.
Perch, White	1 lb.	4 lb., 12 oz.
Perch, Yellow	1 lb.	4 lb., 3 oz.
Pickerel, Chain	1-3 lb.	9 lb., 6 oz.
Pike, Northern	2-4 lb.	46 lb., 2 oz.
Sauger	1-2 lb.	8 lb., 12 oz.
Sturgeon	100-200 lb.	468 lb.
Trout, Brook	½ - 2 lb.	14 lb., 8 oz.
Trout, Brown	½ - 4 lb.	35 lb., 15 oz.
Trout, Cutthroat	1-4 lb.	41 lb.
Trout, Golden	½ - 2 lb.	11 lb.
Trout, Lake	3-5 lb.	65 lb.
Trout, Rainbow	1-2 lb.	42 lb., 2 oz.
Walleye	2-5 lb.	25 lb.
Whitefish, Lake	3-4 lb.	14 lb., 6 oz.

Teach a Man to Fish . . .

Leave it to anglers to come up
with some new angles
to an ancient proverb

Give a man a fish and
you feed him for a day.
Teach a man to fish
and you feed him for
a lifetime.

CHINESE PROVERB

Teach a Man to Fish...

GIVE A man a fish and you feed him for a day. Teach him how to fish and he will sit in a boat and drink beer all day.

COOK A man a fish and you feed him for a day, but teach a man to fish and you get rid of him for the whole weekend.

MOTHER TO DAUGHTER ADVICE

GIVE A man a fish, and you feed him for a day. But teach a man how to fish, and he'll be dead of mercury poisoning inside of three years.

CHARLES HAAS

GIVE A man a fish, and you feed him for a day; give him a religion, and he'll starve to death while praying for a fish.

CATCH A man a fish, and you can sell it to him. Teach a man to fish, and you ruin a wonderful business opportunity.

KARL MARX

Give a man a fish and he will eat for a day. Teach a man to fish and he will keep worms in the refrigerator.

JERRY BIGGS

Give a man a fish, and
you feed him for a day.
Teach a man to fish; and
you can sell him fishing
equipment.

Fishing with the Presidents

They may hold the highest office in the land, but they have their priorities straight when it comes to fishing

IN THESE sad and ominous days of mad fortune-chasing, every patriotic, thoughtful citizen, whether he fishes or not, should lament that we have not among our countrymen more fishermen.

GROVER CLEVELAND

FISHING IS great discipline in the equality of men—because all men are equal before fish!

HERBERT HOOVER

Many of the most publicized events of my presidency are not nearly as memorable or significant in my life as fishing with my daddy.

JIMMY CARTER

FISHING IS much more than fish. It is the great occasion when we may return to the fine simplicity of our forefathers.

HERBERT HOOVER

I HAD been fishing one day and had caught a little fish, which I was taking home. I met a soldier in the road, and having always been told at home that we must be good to soldiers, I gave him my fish.

ABRAHAM LINCOLN ON THE WAR OF 1812

I have been so busy out at the Lodge catching fish—there are forty-five thousand out there— I haven't caught them all yet, but I have all pretty well intimidated.

CALVIN COOLIDGE

AS PRESIDENT, I was able to save with the stroke of the pen a hundred million acres of wilderness area in Alaska. This is the kind of thing that is gratifying to a President, but to be on a solitary stream with good friends, with a fly rod in your hand ... is an even greater delight.

JIMMY CARTER

FISHING IS the chance to wash one's soul with pure air, with the rush of a brook or with the shimmer of the sun on blue water.

HERBERT HOOVER

At the outset, the fact should be recognized that the community of fishermen constitutes a separate class or subrace among the inhabitants of the earth.

GROVER CLEVELAND

When fishing saved our country

Every schoolchild learns the legend of George Washington and Valley Forge.

In 1778, The Continental Army camped for the winter along the Schuylkill River in Pennsylvania. The weather was bitterly cold and the men had few supplies, going barefoot and hungry.

Morale was terrible, and soldiers were starting to desert their posts. Things looked grim for the army and our fledgling country.

That's when fishing saved the day!

Harry Emerson Wildes tells the story in his book *Valley Forge*:

Fishing with the Presidents

"Then, dramatically, the famine complete-ly ended. Countless thousands of fat shad, swimming up the Schuylkill to spawn, filled the river. Soldiers thronged the river bank. . . . The cavalry was ordered into the river bed . . . the horsemen rode upstream, noisily shouting and beating the water, driving the shad before them into nets spread across the Schuylkill.

"So thick were the shad that, when the fish were cornered in the nets, a pole could not be thrust into the water without striking fish. . . . The netting was continued day after day . . . until the army was thoroughly stuffed with fish and in addition hundreds of barrels of shad were salted down for future use."

The rest, as they say, is history.

The Wisdom of Fishing

TO GO fishing is the chance to wash one's soul with pure air, with the rush of the brook, or with the shimmer of sun on blue water. It brings meekness and inspiration from the decency of nature, charity toward tackle-makers, patience toward fish, a mockery of profits and egos, a quieting of hate, a rejoicing that you do not have to decide a darned thing until next week. And it is discipline in the equality of men—for all men are equal before fish.

HERBERT HOOVER

After all these years, I still feel like a boy when I'm on a stream or lake.

JIMMY CARTER

LOTS OF PEOPLE committed crimes during the year who would not have done so if they had been fishing.

HERBERT HOOVER

I LIKE to fish because it is totally relaxing. I love the water. I can concentrate and forget all my worries. I count my blessings while fishing.

GEORGE H. W. BUSH

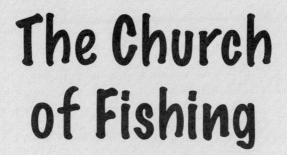

The Church
of Fishing

In the great
cathedral
of all outdoors,
anglers are closer
to Heaven
than most

The Wisdom of Fishing

IN OUR family, there was no clear line between religion and fly fishing. We lived at the junction of great trout rivers in western Montana, and our father was a Presbyterian minister and a fly fisherman who tied his own flies and taught others. He told us about Christ's disciples being fishermen, and we were to assume, as my brother and I did, that all first-class fishermen on the Sea of Galilee were fly fishermen and that John, the favorite, was a dry-fly fisherman.

NORMAN MACLEAN,
A RIVER RUNS THROUGH IT

Some go to church and
think about fishing;
others go fishing and
think about God.

TONY BLAKE

IF FISHING is like religion,
then fly-fishing is high church.

TOM BROKAW

TO HIM, all good things—trout
as well as eternal salvation—come
by grace and grace comes by art
and art does not come easy.

NORMAN MACLEAN,
A RIVER RUNS THROUGH IT

The Church of Fishing

The one thing that a fish
can never find is water;
and the one thing that
man can never find is
God.

ERIC BUTTERWORTH

WHEN A man picks up a fly rod for the first time, he may not know, he has been born again.

JOSEPH D. FARRIS

HEAVEN SEEMS a little closer in a house beside the water.

FISHING IS not a matter of life or death. It's more important than that.

The Church of Fishing

Fishing is Life.
The rest is just
details.

The Fisherman's Prayer

I pray that I may live to fish
Until my dying day,
And when it comes to my last cast,
Then I most humbly pray

When in the Lord's great landing net
And peacefully asleep,
That in His mercy I be judged
Big enough to keep!

God give me strength to catch a fish,
So big that even I,
When telling of it afterwards,
Have no need to lie.

The Best Time to Go Fishing

It's always fishing
time somewhere

TO BE A successful fisherman you should get there yesterday when the fish were biting.

THREE-FOURTHS of the Earth's surface is water, and one-fourth is land. It is quite clear that the good Lord intended us to spend triple the amount of time fishing as taking care of the lawn.

CHUCK CLARK

SINCE THERE is six times as much water as dry land on Earth, any fool can plainly see the good Lord meant for man to fish six times as much as he works.

I spend most of my life
fishing; the rest
I just waste.

There ain't but one time
to go fishin' and that's
whenever you can.

DIRON TALBERT

The two best times to
fish is when it's rainin'
and when it ain't.

PATRICK F. MCMANUS

IF FISHING is interfering with your business, give up your business.

ALFRED W. MILLER

THE BEST time to go fishing is when you can get away.

ROBERT TRAVER

THE WEATHER for catching fish is that weather, and no other, in which fish are caught.

W.H. BLAKE

The Best Time to Go Fishing

WHEN THE wind is in the north
The fisherman goes not forth;
When the wind is in the south
It blows the bait in the fish's mouth;
When the wind is in the east
The fish bite the least.
When the wind is in the west
The fish bite the best.

IN THE morning be first up, and in
the evening last to go to bed, for they
that sleep catch no fish.

ENGLISH PROVERB

The best day to
go fishing is
any day that
ends in a Y.

There's Fly-Fishing, and There's Everything Else

Even fly-fishermen
agree, they are
a breed apart

FLY-FISHING may be a very pleasant amusement, but angling or float fishing I can only compare to a stick and a string, with a worm at one end and a fool at the other.

SAMUEL JOHNSON

FLY-FISHING helps you understand how unimportant your big, real-life problems really aren't.

Fly-fishing is like sex: everyone thinks there is more than there is, and that everyone is getting more than their share.

HENRY KANEMOTO

THERE HE stands, draped in more equipment than a telephone lineman, trying to outwit an organism with a brain no bigger than a breadcrumb, and getting licked in the process.

PAUL O'NEIL

THE DIFFERENCE between fly-fishers and worm dunkers is the quality of their excuses.

FLY-FISHING may well be considered the most beautiful of all rural sports.

FRANK FORESTER

Often, I've been exhausted on trout streams, uncomfortable, wet, cold, briar-scarred, sunburned, mosquito-bitten, but never, with a fly-rod in my hand, have I been unhappy.

CHARLES KURALT

I DON'T KNOW exactly what fly-fishing teaches us, but I think it's something we need to know.

*JOHN GIERACH,
SEX, DEATH, AND FLY-FISHING*

THE ESSENTIALS of a Good Fly-Hook: The temper of an angel and penetration of a prophet; fine enough to be invisible and strong enough to kill a bull in a ten-acre field.

G.S. MARRYAT

Calling fly-fishing a hobby is like calling brain surgery a job.

PAUL SCHULLERY

O, SIR, doubt not that Angling is an art; is it not an art to deceive a trout with an artificial fly?

IZAAK WALTON

FLY-FISHING IS the most fun you can have standing up.

ARNOLD GINGRICH

I HAVE many loves and fly-fishing is one of them; it brings peace and harmony to my being, which I can then pass on to others.

SUE KREUTZER

There's Fly-Fishing and There's Everything Else

IF WE CARRY purism to its logical conclusion, to do it right you'd have to live naked in a cave, hit your trout on the head with rocks, and eat them raw. But, so as not to violate another essential element of the fly-fishing tradition, the rocks would have to be quarried in England and cost $300 each.

JOHN GIERACH

GIVE A man a fish and he'll eat for a day. Teach him to fly fish and he'll move to Montana.

The Wisdom of Fishing

UNLESS ONE CAN enjoy himself fishing with the fly, even when his efforts are unrewarded, he loses much real pleasure. More than half the intense enjoyment of fly-fishing is derived from the beautiful surroundings, the satisfaction felt from being in the open air, the new lease of life secured thereby, and the many, many pleasant recollections of all one has seen, heard and done.

CHARLES F. ORVIS

WHAT A TOURIST terms a plague of insects, the fly fisher calls a great hatch.

PATRICK F. MCMANUS

There is no greater fan
of fly fishing than
the worm.

PATRICK F. MCMANUS

THE ONE GREAT ingredient in successful fly-fishing is patience. The man whose fly is always on the water has the best chance. There is always a chance of a fish or two, no matter how hopeless it looks. You never know what may happen in fly-fishing.

FRANCIS FRANCIS

Some still fish by the strict rules of the river: upstream, dry flies only—and only to rising trout—the sporting way.

THERE ARE very few things in life that are dead center. Three of them are 1955 Ford Pickups, B.B. King, and dry-fly fishing.

JOHN GIERACH

THERE'S A big difference between a dry fly dancing through a riffle and a weighted fur ball dragging on the bottom.

A preference for
dry flies is a choice
of quality
over quantity.

WORK IS for those who do not fly-fish.

THE GREAT charm of fly-fishing is that we are always learning.

THEODORE GORDON

TECHNICAL WORDS and phrases have crept out to fuddle fly-fishing, and the simplicity the small boy and Izaak Walton imparted to the sport is becoming burdened with complexity.

JACK DENTON SCOTT

Trout Fishing in America

A worthy but most
uncooperative opponent

The Wisdom of Fishing

THERE'S NO taking trout with dry breeches.

MIGUEL DE CERVANTES

HERE COMES the trout that must be caught with tickling.

WILLIAM SHAKESPEARE,
TWELFTH NIGHT

ALL THE romance of trout fishing exists in the mind of the angler and is no way shared by the fish.

HAROLD F. BLAISDELL

I am not against golf,
since I cannot but
suspect it keeps armies
of the unworthy from
discovering trout.

PAUL O'NEIL

The Wisdom of Fishing

IF THERE is ever a revolution, trout and salmon fisherman will be the first to go up against the wall. Black bass and bream fisherman will either be in the audience or the firing squad.

RUSSELL CHATHAM

TO MY PURIST trout fishing friends, bass are lowly green fish and brown fish. To me, bass are bent rods and aching arms. To my ex-wife, bass are the bewilderment of addiction.

JIM SLINSKY

Bass Fishermen vs. Trout Fishermen

Bass fishermen watch Monday night football, drink beer, drive pickup trucks and prefer noisy women with big breasts. Trout fishermen watch MacNeil-Lehrer, drink white wine, drive foreign cars with passenger-side air bags and hardly think about women at all. This last characteristic may have something to do with the fact that trout fishermen spend most of the time immersed up to the thighs in ice-cold water.

NEW YORKER MAGAZINE

The Wisdom of Fishing

THERE ARE trout in my river whose
    attitudes,
Are quite of the blackest ingratitude;
Though I offer them duns,
Most superior ones,
They maintain a persistent Black
    Gnatitude.

ENJOY THY stream oh, harmless
fish, And when an angler for his dish,
Through gluttony's vile sin,
Attempts—a wretch—to pull thee out
God give thee strength, oh, gentle trout,
To pull the rascal in.

PETER PINDAR

These brook trout will
strike any fly you present,
provided you don't
get close enough
to present it.

DICK BLALOCK

ALL OF US search for that perfect trout stream. Those who find it treasure it the rest of their lives. Those who don't keep on searching.

JIMMY D. MOORE,
TROUT STREAMS I'VE KNOWN

It's Called Fishing, Not Catching

There's a good reason for that

AN OPTIMIST is a fisherman who takes along a camera.

THERE ARE two kinds of fishermen: those who fish for sport, and those who catch something.

IT IS not a fish until it is on the bank.

IRISH PROVERB

It's Called Fishing, Not Catching

There is no use in your
walking five miles to fish
when you can depend
on being just as
unsuccessful
near home.

MARK TWAIN

ONLY AN extraordinary person would purposely risk being outsmarted by a creature, often less than twelve inches long, over and over again.

JANNA BIALEK

IT HAS ALWAYS been my private conviction that any man who pits his intelligence against a fish and loses has it coming.

JOHN STEINBECK

If we would have caught one more, we would have had one.

The Wisdom of Fishing

YOU DON'T always have to catch fish to have a good day fishing.

SIMON PETER saith unto them, "I go a fishing." They say unto him, "We also go with thee." They went forth, and entered into a ship immediately; and that night they caught nothing.

JOHN 21:3

AND I think, as I angle for fish,
In the hope that my hooks will
     attach'em,
It's delightfully easy to fish—
But harder than blazes to catch'em."

WALLACE IRWIN

The Power of Positive Fishing

Every angler will tell you
that fishing cures everything

THE GODS do not deduct from man's allotted span the hours spent in fishing.

BABYLONIAN PROVERB

ALL GOOD fishermen stay young until they die, for fishing is the only dream of youth that does not grow stale with age.

J.W. MULLER

If people concentrated
on the really important
things in life, there'd be a
shortage of fishing poles.

DOUG LARSON

THERE IS certainly something in fishing that tends to produce a gentleness of spirit, a pure serenity of mind.

WASHINGTON IRVING

TEN YEARS from now I plan to be sitting here, looking out over my land. I hope I'll be writing books, but if not, I'll be on my pond fishing with my kids. I feel like the luckiest guy I know.

JOHN GRISHAM

Fishing is a test of
character, but it's a test
you can take over
as many times as
you want.

JOHN GIERACH

The Wisdom of Fishing

Even a bad day
of fishing
is better than
a good day
of work.

The Power of Positive Fishing

Whoever said
"A bad day of fishing
is better than a good
day at work"
never had their
boat sink.

THE CHARM of fishing is that it is the pursuit of what is elusive but attainable, a perpetual series of occasions for hope.

JOHN BUCHAN

ALL THE charm of the angler's life would be lost but for these hours of thought and memory. All along the brook, all day on lake or river, while he takes his sport, he thinks. All the long evenings in camp, or cottage, or inn, he tells stories of his own life, hears stories of his friend's lives, and if alone calls up the magic of memory.

W.C. PRIME

The Power of Positive Fishing

FISHING IS much more than casting and retrieving and playing your catch. It's the wind in your face, and the sound of wakening birds as the sun peeks over the horizon. It's discovering the magic in each new place and unlocking the mysteries that lurk above and below the surface.

DAVE CASANDA

FISHING IS worth any amount of effort and any amount of expense to people who love it, because in the end you get such a large number of dreams per fish.

For the rich,
there is therapy.
For the rest of us,
there is fishing!

Why Go Fishing?

If you have
to ask, you
don't fish

The Wisdom of Fishing

THE TRAVELER fancies he has seen the country. So he has, the outside of it at least; but the angler only sees the inside. The angler only is brought close, face to face with the flower and bird and insect life of the rich riverbanks, the only part of the landscape where the hand of man has never interfered.

CHARLES KINGSLEY

FISHING SEEMS to be the favorite form of loafing.

EDGAR WATSON HOWE

Why Go Fishing?

Many men
go fishing
all their lives
without knowing
that it is not fish
they are after.

HENRY DAVID THOREAU

I FISH not because I regard fishing as being terribly important, but because I suspect that so many of the other concerns of men are equally unimportant, and not nearly so much fun.

JOHN VOELKER

FISHING GIVES you a sense of where you fit in the sceme of things—your place in the universe. . . . I, mean, here I am, one small guy with a fishing pole on this vast beach and out there in the blue expanse of ocean are these hundreds of millions of fish . . . laughing at me.

JUSTIN RHODES WILKINS

Angling is
extremely
time-consuming.
That's sort of the
whole point.

TOM MCGUANE

I STILL don't know why I fish or
why other men fish, except we like it
and it makes us think and feel.

RODERICK HAIG-BROWN

FISHING IS such great fun,
I have often felt that it really
ought to be done in bed.

JOHN VOELKER

Why Go Fishing?

I FISH because I love to; because I love the environs where trout are found, which are invariably beautiful, and hate the environs where crowds of people are found, which are invariably ugly; . . . because, in a world where most men seem to spend their lives doing things they hate, my fishing is at once an endless source of delight and an act of small rebellion; because trout do not lie or cheat and cannot be bought or bribed or impressed by power, but respond only to quietude and humility and endless patience; . . . because only in the woods can I find solitude without loneliness; because bourbon out of an old tin cup always tastes better out there.

JOHN VOELKER

The Wisdom of Fishing

Great Fishing Songs

1. *I'm Gonna Miss Her* by Brad Paisley
   Best line: "Said I would have to choose/If I hit that fishin' hole today/She'd be packing all her things/And she'd be gone by noon./Well, I'm gonna miss her."

2. *Betty's Got a Bass Boat* by Pam Tillis
   Best line: "Oh, but things sure got a lot better since Betty got a bass boat."

3. *Fishin'* by Elvin Bishop
   Best line: "I'm going fish fish fishin' just to ease my mind."

4. *The Five Pound Bass* by Robert Earl Keen Jr.
   Best line: "The early birdie always gets his worm/Me I always get my wish/When you're talking 'bout that five pound bass son. The early wormy gets the fish."

5. *Catfish Boogie* by Tennessee Ernie Ford
   Best line: "The bobber jumped when mister whiskers hit/My gal flipped and throwed a fit/She pulled and tugged and yelled, what's wrong/I said, baby he's a big and that cat's real gone."

Fishing Widows

No one has
suffered more
(or been more
understanding)
than the wife
of an angler

The Wisdom of Fishing

MY WIFE asked me to go fishing instead of hunting. She said, "We only have white wine."

DANA HAWKES

DO YOU really believe your husband when he tells you he goes fishing every weekend?" asked Joyce's friend. "Why shouldn't I?" Joyce replied. "Well, maybe he is having an affair." "That's impossible; he never comes home with any fish!"

Fishing Widows

A man can't wait
ten seconds for his wife
but he can wait all day
for a fish.

The Wisdom of Fishing

MY WIFE says I'm hard of hearing. All husbands who have been around the block a time or two, know it's called "selective hearing." I hear what I want to hear. I can hear a trout rise. I can hear a spinner hit the water. I can hear the drumming of a grouse at half a mile, but I danged well can't hear her when she wants me to make the bed, or paint the house, etc. etc. I secretly had my hearing tested just to be sure. The doc says it is great, a seven percent loss in my left ear and a ten percent loss in my right. Very typical of anyone who does a lot of hunting with a shotgun. But I'm not about to tell my wife that.

JIMMY D. MOORE

Fishing Widows

If a man is truly blessed,
he returns home from
fishing to be greeted by
the best catch of his life.

Rest in Peace

This past fall I was fishing "The Pool" on a small river in Cape Breton, Nova Scotia for Atlantic Salmon. I need not say where, as we all know "The Pool," and its reputation. A number of bright, large salmon had moved in overnight and the fishing promised to be memorable.

When I arrived, I noticed only one other person. He was an older gentleman, in his seventies I speculated, and he had just started down the pool. His casts were long and graceful with so little effort. The rhythm of his movements and the beauty of the scene were hypnotic. His experience and dedication to the art were obvious and I was moved to sit quietly on the bank and just watch. After five or six casts, and on his last retrieve, there was a huge swirl of water and we both saw the dorsal fin of what was surely a 20-lb. Atlantic Salmon.

Fishing Widows

I knew from previous experience that this was a taking fish, likely to be hooked on the next cast. Just then however, a funeral procession started across the bridge about seventy yards downstream. The elderly gentleman reeled in his line and stepped out of the water. He stood at military attention with his rod smartly at his side and doffed his cap waiting there until the slow procession passed across the bridge and out of sight. He quickly replaced his cap and began stripping line as he made his way back into the water.

I was moved by this display and yet curious. I approached the gentleman and remarked that he must have known the deceased quite well to have possibly lost the opportunity to hook and land the large fish he had raised. He replied "Yes, and if she had lived until next Tuesday, we would have been married fifty-three years."

BOB BOUDREAU

An angler is a man
who spends rainy days
sitting around on the
muddy banks of rivers
doing nothing because
his wife won't let him
do it at home.

You Don't Have to be Crazy, But It Helps

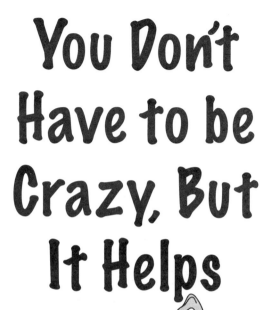

In their hearts,
anglers know
they're right

I GUESS you have to remember that those who don't fish often see those of us who do as harmlessly strange and sort of amusing. When you think about it, that might be a fair assessment.

JOHN GIERACH,
SEX, DEATH, AND FLY-FISHING

FISHING IS only an addiction if you're trying to quit.

I ONCE gave up fishing, it was the most terrifying weekend of my life.

There's a fine line
between fishing and
standing on the shore
like an idiot.

STEVEN WRIGHT

If people don't
occasionally walk away
from you shaking their
heads, you're doing
something wrong.

JOHN GIERACH

The 5 Finest Fishing Films

The next best thing to fishing is watching it

#5
The Old Man and the Sea (1958)
Starring Spencer Tracy
Directed by John Sturges

10-SECOND VERSION:
Desperate fisherman lands a giant
marlin after a three-day battle; sharks
eat it on the way home.

SYNOPSIS:

A luckless fisherman risks everything when
he sails out into the gulf and battles to land
a giant marlin. His quest is ultimately fu-
tile, but the fisherman looks within himself to confront his own frailties. This film
is based on the Ernest Hemingway classic
about man's struggle against nature and his
own inner demons.

FISHING RATING:

#4

Moby Dick (1956)
Starring Gregory Peck,
Orson Welles, Richard Basehart
Directed by John Huston

10-SECOND VERSION:
Fish bites man, man chases fish,
fish kills man and sinks the boat.

SYNOPSIS:
The ship *Pequod* sails out of New Bedford to hunt whales. The crewmen find themselves partners in Captain Ahab's obsessive pursuit of Moby Dick, the great white whale that maimed him. Ahab's madness leads his crew to disaster, and all save one are drowned when Moby Dick sinks the ship. The screen adaptation of Herman Melville's 1851 symbolic masterpiece was written by Ray Bradbury.

FISHING RATING:

★ ★ ★

#3

Jaws (1975)
Starring Roy Scheider,
Richard Dreyfuss, Robert Shaw
Directed by Steven Spielberg

10-SECOND VERSION:
Shark bites people; shark bites boat;
shark blows up.

SYNOPSIS:

The police chief, the young oceanographer and the crusty old fisherman join forces to rid resort town Amity Island of the great white shark that has been terrorizing beachgoers. Once Richard Dreyfuss convinces the others that it is indeed a great white causing the problem, the three end up in a deadly struggle before killing the giant fish.

FISHING RATING:

 ★ ★ ★

#2
Man's Favorite Sport? (1963)
Starring Rock Hudson,
Paula Prentiss, Jim Hutton
Directed by Howard Hawks

10-SECOND VERSION:
Man pretends to know how to fish, enters contest, catches fish, gets the girl.

SYNOPSIS:
The boss of an Abercrombie & Fitch fishing expert enters him in a fishing contest—but nobody knows he's never caught a fish in his life. With the help of a know-it-all Indian and a ditzy chick, Willoughby wins the contest and gets the girl.

FISHING RATING:

#1

A River Runs Through It (1992)
Starring Brad Pitt, Tom Skerritt
Directed by Robert Redford

10-SECOND VERSION:
Father dominates sons, boys act out, family finds love through fishing.

SYNOPSIS:
An emotionally distant minister raises two sons: a scholarly one who settles down, and the handsome, daring one who becomes a journalist. These very different brothers are brought together by a shared love of fly-fishing given to them by their father. One brother's charmed life is destroyed by alcohol and gambling, and fishing becomes a metaphor for their father's unexpressed love.

FISHING RATING:
★ ★ ★ ★ ★

Fishing Gear

If you don't catch any fish, you have to blame it on your gear—and then buy new stuff

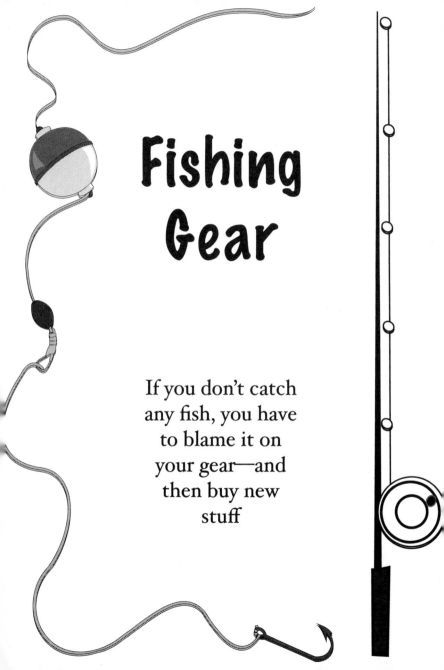

NEVER FORGET that most streams are one inch higher than most hip boots.

ALL YOU NEED to be a fisherman is patience and a worm.

HERB SHRINER

ONCE AN angler has become serious about the sport he'll never again own enough tackle or have enough time to use it."

JOHN GIERACH,
EVEN BROOK TROUT GET THE BLUES

Fishing costs
like sin but requires
heavier clothing.

L.C. CLOWER

The Wisdom of Fishing

IT MATTERS not how many fish are in the sea . . . if you don't have any bait on your hook.

DIAL WEST

SCHOLARS HAVE long known that fishing eventually turns men into philosophers. Unfortunately, it is almost impossible to buy decent tackle on a philosopher's salary.

PATRICK F. MCMANUS

THE MAN who coined the phrase "Money can't buy happiness" never bought himself a good fly rod!"

REG BAIRD

My biggest worry is that
when I'm dead and gone,
my wife will sell my
fishing gear for what
I said I paid for it.

KOOS BRANDT

ROD: AN attractively painted length of fiberglass that keeps an angler from ever getting too close to a fish.

LINE: SOMETHING you give your co-workers when they ask on Monday how your fishing went the past weekend.

Fishing Gear

MY WIFE SAID I have so many fly rods and reels that I cannot possibly use them all. My reply was that I had rods and reels to fish, rods and reels to tinker with and then my fine crafted rods and reels to "fondle and admire, while dreaming of trout fishing during the cold winter months. You can imagine what kind of look she gave me.

JIMMY D. MOORE

The Wisdom of Fishing

A FISHERMAN will spend almost as much time in tackle shops as he will upon a trout stream.

WILLIAM HJORTSBERG

YOUR OUTFIT may be elaborate, or it may be a cane pole. Fortunately, the size of your kit is no indication of the pleasure you derive.

JACK RANDOLPH

IF YOU NEED a piece of equipment and don't buy it, you pay for it even if you don't have it.

HENRY FORD

Ancient Proverbs

Anglers have
been fishing since
the day after fish
were created

HE FISHES well who uses a golden hook.

ROMAN PROVERB

THROW A lucky man into the sea, and he will come up with a fish in his mouth.

ARAB PROVERB

LISTEN TO the sound of the river and you will get a trout.

IRISH PROVERB

To climb a tree
to catch a fish
is talking much
and doing nothing.

CHINESE PROVERB

IN THE pool where you least expect it, there will be a fish.

ROMAN PROVERB

ONE CAN think of life after the fish is in the canoe.

HAWAIIAN PROVERB

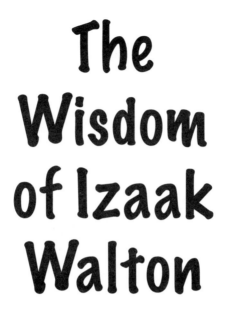

The Wisdom of Izaak Walton

Walton's 1653 book *The Compleat Angler* has remained in print nearly five hundred years

Izaak Walton

Izaak Walton (1593–1683) is often called the father of modern fishing.

His handbook, *The Compleat Angler,* is a classic guide to the pleasures of fishing. First published in 1653, it tells of three friends—an angler, a hunter, and a fowler—story of who travel the countryside discussing their favorite pastimes. It combines a fishing manual, an exploration of folklore, meditations on nature, and songs, ballads, and quotations from several writers.

The Compleat Angler is one of the most reprinted books in history, with more than three hundred editions.

The Wisdom of Izaak Walton

As no man is
born an artist,
so no man is
born an angler.

The Wisdom of Fishing

[ANGLING] deserves commendations . . . it is an art worthy the knowledge and practice of a wise man.

ANGLING may be said to be so like the mathematics that it can never be fully learnt.

RIVERS AND the inhabitants of the watery elements are made for wise men to contemplate.

The Wisdom of Izaak Walton

If I might be judge,
God never did make a
more calm, quiet,
innocent recreation
than angling.

DOUBT NOT but angling will prove to be so pleasant that it will prove to be, like virtue, a reward to itself.

YOU WILL find angling to be like the virtue of humility, which has a calmness of spirit and a world of other blessings attending upon it.

The Final Word

An assortment of
the best fishing
wisdom

A GOLFER has one advantage over the fisherman; he doesn't have to show anything to prove his success.

CATCH-AND-RELEASE fishing is a lot like golf. You don't have to eat the ball to have a good time.

EVEN A fish wouldn't get into trouble if he kept his mouth shut.

Fishing seems to be
divided, like sex, into
three unequal parts:
anticipation and
recollection and,
in between, actual
performance.

ARNOLD GINGRICH

THE CURIOUS thing about fishing is you never want to go home. If you catch something you can't stop. If you don't catch anything you hate to leave.

GLADYS TUCKER

THE SCIENCE of fishing can be had from books; the art is learned by the catching and losing of fish.

W.H. BLAKE, BROWN WATERS

FISHING . . . is a sport invented by insects and you are the bait.

P.J. O'ROURKE

Women break
your hearts, big fish
also break your line
along with it.

FISHING IS the sport of drowning worms.

ALL AMERICANS believe that they are born fishermen. For a man to admit to a distaste for fishing would be like denouncing mother-love and hating moonlight.

JOHN STEINBECK

CAUTION IS a most valuable asset in fishing, especially if you are the fish.

The Final Word

LIFE IS A lot like fishing. The fish (usually) bite when you're not staring at the bobber. However, be ready to reel in your catch when it bites! Kick back, and just let what's supposed to happen, happen. Take initiative when it's time. You the fisher can choose your fishing hole, the bait, and the time you cast out . . . the fish choose when to bite, and then it is up to you as to whether or not you reel it in, or let it get away from you. Much like life I say! Make your cast, then be patient, wait for a bite, then by all means, reel in *your* catch.

JUSTIN RHODES WILKINS

THERE IS only one theory about angling in which I have perfect confidence, and this is that the two words, least appropriate to any statement, about it, are the words "always" and "never."

LORD EDWARD GREY,
FLY-FISHING

OUR TRADITION is that of the first man who sneaked away to the creek when the tribe did not really need fish.

RODERICK HAIG-BROWN

All men
are equal
before fish.

The Wisdom of Fishing

WITH EVERY trip I collect new mementos, though few are collected in scrapbooks. And all who fish for bass across the land collect them too. They are the images from first light to last and from first fish to last. And we'd share them in a minute. Some recall particular triumphs, often preserved in snapshots and clippings, while others we tend to hide, at least until the time we're ready to laugh about them. Daybreaks, canebrakes, heartbreaks, muggy nights, and foggy mornings. A hundred things that worked, and a thousand more that should have. That's bass fishing.

GEORGE KRAMER

The Final Word

APRIL 1ST, 1878 - Opening day. Banks more than full of roily snow water; weather decidedly cold; strong wind from the Northwest; cloudy sky. Managed to fall into the Ogden brook. Reached home in the evening, cold, wet, tired and hungry. Nevertheless, had a most glorious time.

A. NELSON CHENEY

THERE ARE fishing tournaments, contest and pools, to be sure, but . . . by far the most rewarding forms of competition in angling are those that take place between the fish and the angler, and within the angler himself.

JAMES WESTMAN

Fishing is not a hobby.
A hobby is something
you do in your
spare time!

The Wisdom of Fishing

AN OLD MAN in his final breaths called in his family and said, "I must apologize to you all. I suppose I haven't been the perfect father and husband. I shamefully admit that I spent as much of my life as I could in the woods and on the streams. I was rarely at home during the fishing seasons and I'll admit that I spent too much time at the fly shop, and too much money on rods and lines and reels." He paused here to rest for a minute, then continued. "I've been a terrible father and I hope you all forgive me." Then he paused again and looked around. Then he closed his eyes and smiled and said in a half-whisper to himself, "and on the other hand . . . I have caught a helluva lot of trout."

Index

B

C

F

G

H

I

Irving, Washington 80
Irwin, Wallace 76

J

Jerome, Jerome K. 10
Johnson, Samuel 48

K

Kanemoto, Henry 49
Kingsley, Charles 88
Kramer, George 140
Kreutzer, Sue 54
Kuralt, Charles 51

L

Larson, Doug 79
Lincoln, Abraham 22

M

Maclean, Norman 32, 34
Marquis, Don 6
Marryat, G.S. 52
Marx, Karl 16
McGuane, Tom 91
McManus, Patrick F. 43,
    56, 57, 116

Miller, Alfred W. 44
Moore, Jimmy D. 70, 98, 119
Muller, J.W. 78

O

O'Neil, Paul 50, 65
O'Rourke, P.J. 134
Orvis, Charles F. 56

P

Pindar, Peter 68
Prime, W.C. 84

R

Randolph, Jack 120

S

Schullery, Paul 53
Scott, Jack Denton 62
Shakespeare, William 64
Shriner, Herb 114
Slinsky, Jim 66
Steinbeck, John 74, 136

About the author

Christopher Armour has a lifelong love of the outdoors. He is president of Armour&Armour Advertising. Before founding the full-service agency, he worked at *The Tennessean* in Nashville in a variety of positions including sportswriter.

Armour is a 1978 graduate of Yale University. His wife Jan is his partner in the firm. She can bait her own hook.

For more information, contact
Foxglove Press
939 Camp Nakanawa Road
Crossville, TN 38571
1-877-205-1932